Selected Poems

Selected Poems
JEAN EARLE

SEREN BOOKS

SEREN BOOKS is the book imprint of
Poetry Wales Press Ltd
Andmar House, Tondu Road
Bridgend, Mid Glamorgan

British Library Cataloguing in Publication Data
Earle, Jean
    Selected Poems
    I. Title
    821.914

ISBN 1-85411-030-6

Cover painting: 'Chasse au tigre' by Jean-Baptist
Guiraud

*Published with the financial support of the
Welsh Arts Council*

Typeset in 11 point Palatino by Megaron, Cardiff
Printed by Dotesios Printers Ltd, Trowbridge

Contents

New Poems

from A Trial of Strength

from The Intent Look

from Visiting Light

NEW POEMS

Blondie

Most days, this wild weather,
Our bus picks up a girl
Whose splendid hair lights up the rattling box,
Trespasses, undrawn,
Over the back of her seat.

Ideal beauty — Helen's or Isolde's —
How can we be sure
These timeless ladies' lure
Was blonde and beautiful?
Because the torch of it lives on
In everyman's blood,
Continuing fire.

I have seen a man,
Sitting behind, advance trembling fingers,
Seemingly unaware
Of his mesmerised touch

As when the monks dug up
Arthur and Guinevere, that queen
Lay with her great yellow plaits unfaded —
So their fascinated hands
Must have presumed.

She comes to her stop,
Hurries the shining mane
Cometwise through the bus. Thuds down.
Wind and rain ravel the gold across
Her pudding face.

Chocolate

(for Libs)

Now the affair's done — no substance left —
I nibble dark on chocolate, day and night.
Because you're gone, my deprivation sucks
Chocolate, instead of you. Those wild enzymes
Love hots the blood with —
Chocolate has the same
Physical addiction. Oh, how I lunge
Towards my fix,
In its red-gold pack! I had a dress like that
When we went dancing. Now I'm fat
From my hopeless binge, and will never, never
Wear it again. Love, would you know me now
I'm a chocolate junkie — spotty
And fat — fat — *fat*?

Devil's Blackberries

Late pickers — cut off from sunset
In a ditch of brambles —
From earthed heels let fly
Their lengthening shadows

That shoot up the hill behind,
To a view of the sea.

Far from their source,
These poles-with-pinheads
Stripe on the glowing slope
Personalities
All their own. Pity they have no eyes,
Since they are here, to watch
The passionate tide blooding the coast.

The sun goes down, the gatherers creep
Out from the thorns,
Their shadows come to heel.

No one has put the sunset
To any use. Over the hill
The group bedraggles home
Shadows that go before them,
Berries. And worms.

The Amaryllis

Its opening mouth
Sucks at the pane, its soaring bud
Aims at a sun too far
Above this potbound house.
The calyx turns
Always away from us,
Towards more light....

And so we cannot appraise
Its situation, without going outside
To look. We are too diffident
To stand, openly gazing
At a personal blaze.

The truth is,
This vivid cry is not the sort of thing
Our village sets in a window.
People pass,
Glancing elsewhere. Now there's a boy
Slowing his bike as though intrigued
By the catchsight.
He is of an age
Not to acknowledge challenge to the eye
Though the blood jumps at it.
He wobbles on....

Only tonight,
When curtains must be drawn
Against indecisions —
And there may be frost —
Shall we shift this splendour into our midst,
Assess the odds
Against it lasting out, before time's thirst
Darkens and slacks its fire.

We'll stare down
Unfurling corollas
Into the white heart
Of all we might become, if we understood
Fully, and by the giant light
Such growth demands,
What we'd be taking on.

Jugged Hare

She mourned the long-ears
Hung in the pantry, his shot fur
Softly dishevelled. She smoothed that,
Before gutting — yet she would rather
Sicken herself, than cheat my father
Of his jugged hare.

A tender lady, freakish as the creature —
But resolute. She peeled it to its tail.
Oh, fortitude! Her rings sparked in and out
Of newspaper wipes. Blood in a bowl,
Sacrificial gravy. A rarely afforded
Bottle of port.

She sustained marriage
On high events, as a child plays house.
Dramas, conciliations —
Today, the hare. She sent me out
To bury the skin,
Tossed the heart to the cat.

She was in full spate.

Fragrance of wine and herbs
Blessed our kitchen; like the hare's dessert
Of wild thyme; or like his thighs
As though braised by God. She smiled
And dished up on willow,
Having a nice touch in framing
One-off scenarios.

After the feast, my father was a lover
Deeply enhanced.
I heard them go to bed,
Kissing — still inside her picture.
Later, I heard her sob
And guessed it was the hare
Troubled her. My father slept,
Stunned with tribute. She lay now
Outside her frame, in the hare's dark

Hating her marital skills
And her lady-hands, that could flense a hare
Because she wooed a man.
In years to come,
I understood.

In the Great Oak

Boy's voice,
Shouting obscenities
Inside the territory of this oak —
Against your short-lived noise
An oak is immortal.

Crown overhang
Pegs down perimeters
Structured like mastodon's ribs
Or a king's house
From which you monkey-dangle,
Bellowing your jibes.

An acorn falls.

Your smut shrills
Over the spent of twigs,
Fungi, shadows.....
Stirs up delicate flies
That go down with the sun.
Your ego bawls....

The other boys sneak home
But you rave on.

Watch it!
In autumn, the Green Man,
In a bush for priest-cloak,
Prowls this circuit, tracking
Such potent zest.

He does as he must
For life's renewal. You — crude voice —
Osiris, the young Adonis,
The nourishing Christ.

What Shall We Do To Be Saved?

Poetry's indignations —
What can they achieve
Except elegies

For the world of trees
Shrinking before fire,
For dispossessed
Wing, fur, flower —
More decent and more lovely
Than ourselves.....

Gone: and will not alert now
Any coming eye.

Poetry-with-music, once
Was a shield against enemies....

No more.

Rather, the visual arts
Itch at us. Guernicas,
Unknown political prisoners,
Nature films, where move
Things from our fathers' childhood.
Fairytales.

Vision, for most of us,
Is difficult. Goodwill tires
Of the long red News,
The green funerals. We cling
To home in a cul-de-sac,
Seldom intend
Beyond the cupressus.

Always, the powers to cleanse
Troll their thick seas, their acrid airs,
Under flags of convenience.

"Things will last our time....."

But now, the softly whorled
Shell of the globe

Splits

Showing the Sun in Nakedness.

His lasers scorch us.
Almost — it might be said —
Honour, to absorb
The prophesied burn....

Molten he bids for us.
Of such integrity
His takeover would be,
His reconstructions
Lethally pure. Oh man — for once, for once
Nothing to do with money.

In a Train

Two. Alone

Although, opposite,
Travelled a third.

His arm around,
her palm on his knee...

Very pretty; had bought little boots
And was pleased. Tried one on,
Turning her foot
Pliant in his hand.

Went to sleep
Against his neck. His body curved,
Rhyming with hers.
She was easy to read, the third traveller's
Unobtrusive scan had her by heart.
But he?

Boy as he was, a macho beard
Masked how, to worldly eye, the lower face
Forecasts the man.

Bright, as they flew,
Water beside the track — and something moved
On its surface.
Rising? Drowning?

The third passenger's
Peripatetic glance
Couldn't decide. Whatever she had glimpsed
Seemed related to those two — but how?

Her mind retained only a keen ripple
Widening out and out.

Out....and out......

The Flip Side

On first waking — a wing-brush,
Trying the window. But day's white
Pales this prediction.
Beds fling apart
Pillows and silence,
The threat recedes
For now, trapped into sheets,
Into hands as they button and zip
And let go....
For an open grasp is required
With toast, essential outcries,
Jolly goodbyes.

But then....

Virginia Woolf saw a black fin
Crossing the ocean of her day.
She was committed, lost,
It was her sign, a ticket
To darkness; not to be trapped
Into any hand.

What is this wing, or fin,
Trailing a wisp
Through the lake of sight —
Floater, or veil,
Deepest eclipse,
A migraine's clout?

Often, it is a lining
To pure happiness — the flip side.
To be expected, endured,
Even gloried in
After some magical use
Of the spirit's eye

Which has to be paid for
In weight and kind
Matching the delight.

As all gifts must.

The Jackdaw

A chancy morning, after rain.

Cot-child opening
To differences in light, words —

Which clump together now
Muscular knots, lifting the infant head,
All eyes, all ears.

A voice in the lane,
Calling through misted sun.
"The jackdaw's dead."

Never to know whose voice,
Which bird; that lane
Viewed from a window only.

No one there.

Often, piercing the long life's
Deep experience
Of rain silvering a bright sun

These claps: without any reference
To what's being said, what's on.....
Like a spoke in a wheel,
Suddenly it squeaks
Out of a radiant fog.

"The jackdaw's dead."

In the Night

When we were children, out to tea,
The child of the house showed us his toys,
Their glancing novelties
And fit loveliness to do as he said.

He was beautiful too; elegant as a bird
Up trees and over walls. He had acquired techniques
Far beyond our stodge of childishness.

We riffled his books; bright pictures, cruel stories,
Taxed our understanding. Then, he was sarcastic.
He stood in a puddle and stamped —
Dirt — and rainbows —
Flew all over our clean dresses.

He invited us to the top of the house
And shut us in the dark attic.

Such an entertainer! Yet, never once
Did he look straight at us — merely put on his tricks,
Miracles of display. Considering, in particular,
The attic — I have wondered, sometimes,
Whether God is not like that boy?

But He tells me, He is not. In the night He tells me,
When it is often imperative to know.
A felled tree once assured me
He is to be trusted —
And a film where the crocodile carried her eggs
In her jaws, so tenderly, without hurting any
Against the craters of her terrible snap.

It must be fault in myself, how seldom
Anything human convinces me
God is not like that boy....

Young Girls Running

Almost, flight.....

Herons, angling
A tilted grace. Spring twigs,
Taking the awkward wind.

Three-as-one, linked onrush
Mirrored in polished sand,
Light legs
Spattering pools, shells.

"The sea!" they cry, "the sea!"
Birdlike, birdshape

Breasting the tide
With no breasts, merged
In the thrown wave

Which will rain them
Rosy, swept
Through its firming sting,
Medicinal shock, thrust...

They will be women,
Breasted, hipped,
Salted,
When they come out.

The Pole Star

Why don't these crocuses delight you
As they do me? Look at them again.
Scarcely could we set a pin between
Yet each finds room to quiver as though pulsed
In rhythm with our blood.
Surely you can receive
This gift with more than a bent brow's
Kind inattention? I feel like a child
Snubbed by a friend!

And yet — how often have you shown
How to locate the Pole Star...
I gaping up, disorientated,
Pecking at the dark

As, with endurance, I have watched
The bow of your spine
Relax in pleasure, after some true shot
Into abstractions you find beautiful.

To me, closed.....

Save that I see (a gleam in and out)
How what moves you may be another form
Of the crocus? Light is interchangeable
With light. You tolerate
My fevered springs; and though I spin so lost
In the night sky

I respect your Pole Star.

Ynys Lochtyn

Stone face
Asleep between tumblerocks
Jagged along the sea.

High cliffs look down.

We dream
Across drowsiness. Pools wink
Lights and creatures over the smooth
Tide-floors, stretching away
To the stone sleeper. The sun's course
Changes him. Now his chin juts
Into afternoon; but the sealed lids
Hush every glare
Into fermenting yesterday
And tense tomorrow. Slopes braze
Purple and gold, a mist gauzes
Coherent thought.....

Yet it becomes
Hazily sure — this monumental face,
Wedged fast by time and the sea's rage,
Slumbers for us; and for all things
Poised above fall. In pools
Trembled with predators; through undercrofts
Of heather and furze,
Shaken by the wind

And in our resting minds —
That will recall this face
When we lie down
In other summers. Father's or mother's face,
Whoever was on our side. Dozing with us
When we tired of playing
Or, in a safe house,
Hearing the sea, after the brilliant day.

Strawberry Fields

Hi! the Pensioners' Club, bottoms-up
Along these strawy rows,
Fruited with July.
A dignified few
Cannot or will not bend —
Others show pants
In stooping, heedless as a child.

Almost all are fat.

They turn girls and boys
For an hour's stop. It works miracles.
Grey blood pinks up, they feel the weight
Of a neighbour's haul,
Challenging, sharp.
Some grudge the time to taste
But pick and pick
Obsessively as once they played tag
Or banged football.

Punnets wedged tight,
Now they roll home — fulfilled.
All down the motorway
A following wind
Blabs to the smoggy world,
"Ripe strawberries...."

Till the hot coach demotes
That rosy kiss to a pervading bruise —
Heavy; and hard to take
Till the trip's end —
Of funeral wreaths.

A Cloud Above Towy

Waiting a bus.

Everyone tired with February,
Everyone damp
From the last shower.

Moon full but pale —
It is still teatime light.

This Cloud Person passes,
Slow, huge in the cleared sky.
His enormous profile
Looms on the darkening
River valley, his back hair
Fringed with pink. Upon his giant lip
The moon raises a slight smile.

Off, at last,
Nobody cares for his majesty.
Only a child
Peers up. The bus turning
A roundabout, her window fills
With his luminous changesides.
She ponders fish
In the Towy — how, her father jokes,
They fight up from the sea
Simply for him to catch
On a Saturday. But now the Cloud
Bears on their sleep, the water blushes
His trailed rose; and as the moon brightens,

He fades. The child clutches
Important shopping, ready to dart out
And dart in, to her home —
With a faint smiling
Reflected from that source, as by the rising moon
On Cloud-lip.

The Dancing Stone

I had a baby then
And was in deep country. Arduous days
Ended in cunning moves
Toward sleep. I pushed, she rode —
Always awake and laughing —
To a great stone in a field.
There the rabbits danced in the evening.

It was before men saved the fields from them.
Under furze their ring-o'- roses crept
Nor ever emerged; or blundered about,
Senseless to danger, dying of slow obscenities.

Who cared, save such as myself — helpless —
And rabbit trappers?

Perimeters run green now, the full crop
Presses the hedge. I understand
All the advantages: yet the concession brings
Dark convictions. A woman and a child —
If our watching had threatened their fields,
Men with answers would have found a way
Of dealing. Never mind the means....

Old glass, in King's College Chapel —
Unstained, set into a back window —
Shows the Holy Family
New every day. Nothing at all to do
With the high treasures where they also stand,
Jewelling light.

This is how men once looked
On other forms than theirs, that looked with them at Christ.
This etcher flowed his tool straight
From a gentler source, seeing in ox and ass,
Farm dog and fowls — a yearning group —
Kinship of man with animals, their shapes incurved
One with mansoul. And yet, perhaps next day
The butcher came?

No answer comes — now or at any time.
He is centuries dead who etched the Christmas beasts
With a double significance. My daughter's child
Feels and sees nothing, when I sometimes say,
"We used to watch the rabbits
Dancing on a stone — your mother and I."

Shadowland

Obsessed with shadows....

As a child, waking in moonlight,
Learns forever the imprint of his house
On the white lawn.

The man without shadow
Is a vampire. I looked for him
Along all sunny floors
But never found him.

Tonight, though, on thronged platforms,
So many vampirish figures —
All without shadows for the lighting's dim.
The world has become
Neutral to them. Token hunting-rites
Seldom produce a kill, the legalised
Stake through the heart.

In the buffet's womb,
Clutching collapsible
Cartons of scald, I stare out
On crowd-suspects
Burdened with weights of our time,
Dark haversacks....

But see, behind this panel
Of clouded glass, three silhouettes
Casting their muted colours,
Not their shadows.

A small shape clambers the man's legs,
A woman's arm
Blurs along his. They swing their link
Playfully between them — shadowless, and yet
Nothing to do with vampires.

Grant, that these three
Seemingly light travellers
Soon take train; out into glorious day
And its relevant shadows.

The Chimney Bird

Another world up there,
Lid of our box.

He opens his wings — opens —
Not quite ready.
Turns about, flopping
The lice-ridden cup.

Inside our box,
Cooksmoke, mansmoke,
Moneysmoke....
Such fusspot; so many locks.

Dawn lift-off.
He opens his wings — opens —
Not quite steady.

He loops the blue loop!

Great light
Picks every lock

Yet from the lifesmoked beds
Not one looks up.

Merlin's Hill

I

How lovely is the bending of necks
When feeding young....
Even squat shapes will turn a curve
Tenderly deft; even fierce things
Solicitously droop
An arc as pure and true
As mathematics.

On Merlin's Hill, I watched a bird
Day after day bring food
To her grounded nestling. She did this
Still, though her computed term
Prompted the next brooding and new eggs.

There is a girl in the village does so.
Healthy and young, teeming
Rich urgencies, she puts aside
All gifts, to insist life,
Life, to her child who cannot open
The mouth of his mind.

Observer on the Hill, I find so much
Spellbinding food — though the rained earth
Writhes up a mist about its cruel truths
And winter threatens. Mostly, it is
Simply the sustenance of commonplace

As with the ants' rushed migrations,
Carrying pieces of leaves, each like a boat
With sail out. Meanwhile,

To a hut by the road, a man hurries legs
Under offcuts of plywood. What is to choose
Between human vocations,
Ant's and bird's — borrowing Merlin's eye,
At a remove of sight?

II

They say that, years ago,
All Whitsun-white
(For it was Pentecost, Christ had gone up)
The people walked with jam sandwiches
And nettle pop — as picnics were
At that plain time — to drop their pins
In the mislaid well
On Merlin's Hill.

Somewhere here, he lives on —
Merlin; or Arthur or some Roman man,
Who can be sure?
With Vivien, his witch-wife —
Guinevere, Mithras —
Potent companions for death-in-life.

He will rise again.

We still drop pins
From minds conditioned by old tales,
Half-beliefs. Oh, those were easy times
To feel and tell,
Compared with ours....
Walking on picnics, dropping pins of faith

Along the bendy, windy, lonely little roads
On Merlin's Hill.

And we need such stabs
Out of the forerunners; stains of their jam
From the rhubarb patch, coarse bread
Baked in myth's oven. Patriarchal strolls
Across these slopes tattooed
With silos and bungalows.

He shudders, perhaps — Merlin —
Under built-over haulms
Of the Old Peoples,
Under the children's crumbs
And their conjuring pins (in case it's so)
Asking his power to save.

"Someone without faith walks in his training shoes
Over my grave."

III

Bishop Ferrar fled
Over this emerald lump,
Hefting through summer airs
The wrong faith for his time.
'His banner over me'
(Tattered, afraid yet strong)
Dodged through foxglove and fern
To a farm behind Merlin's

Which still stands.

People there would have served him
Ale of compassion, their house bread —
Which the Bishop would have blessed,
Sharing it round, girding himself the while
How, like that Other, he must leave his friends
Very soon. And then, the soldiers came.

A farm legend,
Passed life to life, would preserve Ferrar,
Dealing round the bread.

Where he was burned, in Carmarthen town,
Idlers sit
Watching traffic between Woolworth's
And the Angel Vaults.
They do not think of him.

With Merlin, Arthur, Mithras,
He is long gone.
Over the Hill, his appointment with fire
Stamps like an aerial photograph. His stake
Centres the swifts, screaming at their games
Round Abergwili spire.

Bishop Ferrar's stake is reputed to have been built into the spire
of Abergwili Church.

Demolition

On the exposed wall,
A grate; of that mean size
Sparking an eye for sickness
Or for birth —
Otherwise cold. On its shelf, a vase
Still upright,
Lasting the day's shocks
And the rammer's noise.

Chill in the night and the vase falls.

Who was here?

It was the custom once
To stuff a vase with pluckings
Out of the comb. After long saving
These were dressed and rolled
Into the living hair, as though
Life and upspring, the fullness round the face
As the comb swept, were never lost.
This pad was vanity's trick
And was called "a rat."

Rat-pads of dross
Thicken the sunken floors,
Shore up rooms
Pitted with distressed
Echoes and tints, after the certain
Fall of the vase.
Invisible gaps
Filled in by dust, where shelves have been
And vase-like human shapes...

Hollows for lying down,
For trembling,
Storage of delicate or rough,
Instant and necessary things.

Common spoons, voices....
Through warrens of air
Siffles the world's pavan
For its lost sanctuaries,
Its unrecorded drast.

Who was here?

Menopause

Now and again —
Since I was quite young —
I reckon my quota of seed
That we stopped from growing: not, of course,
All would have made it — there wasn't time
Nor strength in myself. But I think of them.

We raised three — and couldn't really have done
With more. It just feels strange
I might have had a dozen
Persons in my gift: and who would they have been?

In school biology, we were told once
How the female seeds
Are laid down at her making; one to go
Every month, when her body's ready,
Taking its chance.

I remember sniggers — also, myself
Looking from the window
Even as I smirked. What a day it was,
Blue and white...
And the thing seemed wonderful?

Seed by seed, lined up for years,
Waiting in my dark for the blind push
To be someone. More curious to me
Than the well-known puzzles,
Everyone's go. God — the stars...

I don't suppose Jack ever gave a thought
To such ideas. Men are so wasteful,
Careless of their seed. I often guess
What lives those might have had,
Given some luck.

The colours of their eyes...

Late News

As it grows late for me, the future clears
Like a child's eye; but darkness falling
Has fewer stars.

Not going about much, seeing small —
Through the long nights restlessly reviewing
What the life was.....

This knob brings in the world —
Both where I might have gone
If I would and where I would not — no!
Yet here it comes, before I can switch off
The horrors. I use my hand,
Not that indulgent gadget
Whereby my slowed body need not shift
From the chair. So News arrives,
Relentless. On some nights —
However toughened by what the life was —
One seems more vulnerable.

Not to humanity's News — which, nowadays,
Clouts like a whirlwind's blasting violence —
But brief, no-comment items
Which darkness, with fewer stars,
Somehow finds all-important

Such as that Chinese bear, grown so vast
They cannot think how to cope with him.
His nose rootles
The bars, rootles his useless parts,
Sore with his situation and fat longing.

Best not to have watched that!

Tonight the Gulf, glaring indigo,
Vomits bombed oil. Dolphins juggle
Sick bellies, turn their uneasy wheels,
Felloed with pollution.

Fishes, too — the News states, curtly —
Sea snakes..... *'Oh, happy living things,*
Blue, glossy green and velvet black....'
All night, a stew of muck-feathered birds
Stinks against all defence. It takes an old man
Slumped in a chair (no gadget)
To stick his head
In a cushion and cry, "Enough...."

Who now
But the very old, remember when the worst
Evils of humanity occurred
Far from one's centre — when an obscene war,
A violated child, were always somewhere else
Where one was blessed not to be.
Now they are in my home!

I must get a gadget.....

Implications of Sight

The poet, as a boy,
Always came downstairs
Slightly above the treads —
Unobtrusive flying.
Not that it was remarked.
He often thought, "It's odd —
Nobody noticing...."

He, alone.
Alone: for he is apt to see
Not as the world perceives
The world's things.
For him, they plump with darkness,
Potency; or else a diamond frill
To the plainness, all mortalities
Glimmered in gem-light. The eye dies
In a starfall with so much seeing.
And still — who cares?

A gift not for unloading on friends.
Critics, perhaps, may pause to taste
The poet's voices
Bouncing off stones — may gulp some titbit down,
Passing it out like branflakes,
Unprocessed waste, left lying.

As for friends...
Who would wish them the inconvenience
Of seeing, say, a chair
More than a chair, even to madness?
Each and every form invaded, upended,

51

For its prime derivation,
Not for what it is

And this — kills. A friend is better blind
Than seeing so. His range of vision
Being 'A' or 'B', how should his sight survive
The wounding force of 'C'?
Do not disturb. A poet needs friends.

Companions? Ah...

Has the wind a companion?

What the poet asks
For company (but may not face, full-on,
Even with diamond-sight)
Is white authority,
Fletching and homing arrows
Into the world

Such as the poems of Christ....

Or the risen sun,
Day after day after day
Since life began!

Tortelier, piercing with an upward glance
From his cello —

Here and there a sign,
THIS IS THE WAY

But an unmanageable light.

Too much alone,
The poet rests his gaze
In the presence of friends

Who'll read him as they see him —
Crippled.

Nor, in their tactful house,
Will have the loutish manners
Even to question his odd ways
Of coming downstairs.

Honesty

Always a 'snapper-up of trifles' —
Jars from a skip, those rubber bands
Postmen let fly —
Some sad kitten —
After her trip, she brought me such a thing,
A seed of honesty
From Wordsworth's garden.

Had she any idea
How it pleased me? Only as tourist
At Dove Cottage had she ever heard
Of William and Dorothy

Who may well have trodden the soil
This seed sprang from....

Sowing the scarlet beans; or when Dorothy
Set herbs by moonlight. When she worked alone,
Grieving for William — who had taken joy
Of their life together into his stern hold
And gone for Mary.

Intense and ardent hearts! The seed sent up
A thin stalk, has managed a few flowers
Of a sharp magenta. She who stole me this
Finds it not worth the snatch,
Having no clue
How eloquent to me — yes, as a friend's dress
Seen against time and light,
Its colour is.

Dancing Pheasants

Under the white peak,
A watcher.

A naked field where two birds,
Ruby-and-topaz mantles pricked,
Scrape their big feet.

The watcher, frozen; but in bird blood,
Primeval fires.

They dance; and the watcher smiles,
Deep in his snowy heart....
So the near-men
May have learned smiling
When they began to dance
Through watching the birds

That were evolving from dinosaurs.
Shag woods —
So long sunken
Not a fossil returns —
In overlaps of time
Might have concealed both the first men
And the last dragons?

The little dragons
(That were almost birds)
Danced in their spring scales,
Mutive to feathers —
While the monkeyish men
Peered from defensive covers
As men do still.

And they smiled.

What has changed? Not the scrape dance-floor,
The watcher — who has always twitched
His atavistic smile. Huff, puff and burnish —
A formal lust,
Ritualised — pursued
Even to death's bloody bow

While the dun hen, spring after spring,
Loses eggs to the crow.

Myriad transitions, varying only
The outward forms.
No mid-quick changes...

Not cock nature
Nor the hen's steady plan
For the one egg left.

Least of all —
Oh, least of all, first-and-last men.

Re-Reading The Iliad

I touch to stay Hector from his death
As he stands at our gate
To the open road —
Which is busy; and once he leaves our garden
It's another world.

Andromache hastens from our house
Their loved son. She staggers flowers
With her urgent hems. "Dear my lord...."
But the golden child takes fright
At his father's war plumes.

They laugh together; husband and wife
We know,
For the last time.

He puts off his helmet on our lawn,
Lifts the lad to his brown
Reassuring smile.
See the likeness of man and boy
Develop and shine!

Our Hannah runs up, making a mope and cry
At *her* dad's fun.

Antarctica

I

Falklands / Malvinas...

A farmer, staring across wire
To prohibited moors, catches the puff
Of exploding mines where his sheep graze

And sappers, negotiating bluffs
Above the Sound, come upon ruins
Of a soldier; the fretwork of his bones
Scattered towards Antarctica.

Was he theirs or ours?

They cover him under gales
From the last inviolate land, its shadow
Upon the sea, the potent horizon.

He died within its gate,
Thought — if he thought at all —
He died for that,
For principles and rights.

Falklands. Malvinas.

II

Shades of the Children's Newspaper,
Grandfather-time. Chalked names
For our example,

Scarlet on black. Respected tales
Told and re-told. Flags of achievement
And disappointment. From these we learned
How men endure.

Desperate survivals
In the maw of storm. A wave of Hokusai,
Raven above the boat.
Layered in ice, only the diary stored
Private concessions.

"God...
This is an awful place!"

III

Schools'-eye view. How the forms sat
Row upon row, at the cinemas,
Watching their heroes shoot
The ponies and dogs.

Before robots and high technologies.
No need of heroes now — no need,
At last, of men?

*I am going out
And may be a long time.*

IV

Testing. Testing.

Nukeypoo, experimental power station,
Wept at extreme conditions
And was put down.
The hut village — soon abandoned —
Lets in the wind, clatters
Discarded cans, drums roll corrupting force
Against virginities. Polythenes
Whip their entangled sheets,
Sailing the blizzards
Across penguin nurseries.

Man's indestructible trash,
Trapped in the berg's translucence
At seasonal melt,
Penetrates, poisons, migrates afar off
To immaculate goals.

And now, the Treaty lapses.

'Peaceful purposes only,
Observations
Fully exchanged.'

The nations yield each other
Foxy facilities.

Testing, testing...

V

They will reckon her all over, by remote control,
As an eligible bride
Is assessed for the dowry. Scans inserted
Into the noble crowns of her head, echo-sound
Tapping her summer sleep.
They will sense reserves
Of her blue blood, where the krill run
Profitable veins —
Insinuate probes
For costing her intimate places,
Estimating deeps
Of her nature and fierce recoil
From their lust.

Is she worth the try?

VI

They defile, extract, so that the whale starves
And the seal phases out. Greenpeace flies
A distracted banner — brave but vain —
On the raped heart.

Till the day comes (has come already)
When the defective rig
Bursts to the sky, treacling its greasy freeze
Across pure wilderness. The bride lies
In a black dress. It is not her wedding
But her funeral. All her superb

Out-of-bounds estate, her chastity-belt,
Unlocked. Nothing to stage lament
For what she was but that mysterious fire
Greed cannot rule nor science harness yet....
Aurora, lapping its marvellous veils, a screen
Above this manmade death.

Chunnel

They pray in shifts
At the Electronic Drill, manoevring its nerves.
As an organist injects
Huge pipes with groans, so they direct
Plates grinding the chalk; night-and-day eroding
Towards a computed round
Of opposite light.

A temple of technology
Fronts this altar; with but few priests,
Upon whose helmeted hearts
The sea weighs heavy, as their software worms
Remorseless segments, tightening the seal.

Above, in Kent-day,
Tides change, vessels and crews
Pursue familiar marks. That White Cliff,
Reared from diatoms, demonstrates abaft
A raped foreshore of rigs and rails
Marshalled like armies.

Ancient fields
Await despoiling, all the protested way
From the Weald to the Last of England.

'Halfway down
Hangs one that gathers samphire —
Dreadful trade.'

Afterwards

The surviving half of the earth
Shuddered: centred the sun:
Went on turning.

With that year's decline
The migrant birds
Followed their stars
To alternate summer
And the steadied trades
Carried such butterflies and moths
As make these odysseys — mindless
Whether they journeyed as birds or insects

For some were effortless travellers,
Catching a lift, duveted against windwarps
By stronger flyers. Within each skull —
Insect or bird —
Delicate, fierce magnets
Locked on the goal, moving in cloud
Or vee formations,
To the summer land.

Likewise, through immemorial
Byeways of seas, fishes and eels
Urgently pressed towards the birth-rivers.

And there was nothing....

Nesting materials
Nor caterpillars, nor the inherited dance
Of ephemera, nor the expected
Certain alighting places.

The home waters ran no taste
Of arrival. Manifestations of death
Clogged in the bays. By natural law,
No U-turn possible......

They hovered while —
Sensing some predatory cull
More ruthless than usual —
Till the overstretched wings
Weakened and fell. The insect pheromones
Received no messages. On the bad tides
New phosphorescence
Dulled — and stank.

That was the season when there were — for once —
No human predators.

Old Friends

A few together, talking round a fire
Of things unconnected with themselves
Or with 'the world'...

Mood and weather
For such indulgence becomes rare,
High subjects few. Tonight, no wit
Or conversational toys: simply a desire
To move above the storms, mind in mind

Yet smiling too, at dangers of the light
Up there, and easing down to earth.....

Fond of each other still, as when they were
Brief boys and girls.

Static

Stripping off her clothes, in the dark,
Their stuffs flashed out a gentle lightning
About her legs; and being off,
Lay dead.

She thought,
"Is it the essence of myself,
Practising that stroke
When it leaves the head —
Taking the heartbeat with it —
And joins thunder,
Rolling a luminous birth
Out of life's dress?
That will slip — so —
Cling — so —
Flash. And, being off,
Lie dead..."

Escape to Felinganol

I

Remembering escapes,
We smile.
Breath let out
After a risk —
Bird manoevred
Through a dark church
To sunlight.....

Trapped in a burning city.
Heart and hands
Powered indignant, huge —
Conjuring child, mother, cat,
Free of this insult of men's wars

To a pocket of old ways
That ceasefire — when it came —
Would erode forever. I shook my dears
Like toys from a Christmas sack,
Into that house
Snowbound in exquisite silence,
By the well field.

Here, we must work for our fires,
Snapping the bones of beech
Off the white hedge, dousing with paraffin.
The bones flared
Summer colours. The child gazed
And napped. Cat began to wash
And my mother said,
"Where I grew up, we too
Went to a well."

Completing her escape, she smiled.

No water in the bombed house
And none in this,
Unless carried. I took the can
Left for our use — slithered and slipped
Into a path worn from the door
By generations.
Over the well, the stone hood
Was capped in snow. Lightly the water steamed,
Scented with cold — like young, fresh fish
Or fresh leaves or the first frost.

Child dozing, cat settling,
Mother smiling...
We had escaped! Through a white smother
I smiled myself, lugging that water back.
We rammed a kettle on the beech fire
And drank together.

II

I fetched water at any time —
And should not have done.
The field had its theme,
Its rites. Neighbours could not have told me
In words; but moved orderly feet
Each on a way trodden from house to well
By their gone people. This blood link
Processed at proper times; morning and evening
Always. And once on Sundays.

Moonlight was not the time —
Nor afternoon, when the field put on
Its open face of flowers.
Nor should the cat have frisked alongside,
Animals were barred. Nobody crouched,
Like me, to catch the water-light
Under the hood. It was not done
To notice toad migrations
Or the shining damozel shedding her prison
Of skin on the warm stone
(Equivalent of a smile).

I broke all their rules
And went on doing it. Took sorrows there,
And naps. Picked God to pieces —
Hunting odd scraps of Him through the long grass —
Even spread out the child's washing,
Happily tracing colours
Pressed through damp stuffs.
Identities of herbs
Faintly about her
For a shawl, when she wore the garments.

III

Once, at noon, when the field slept
Under its polka-dot of small flowers,
An old woman stood on her family path,
Looking...

I knew who she was —
Strayed from the house where she was dying,
Down to the well.

Child, girl, wife, mother of sons
And slow widow...
At the proper times, morning and evening...

But now was noon. The field offered her
Scents and airs, smiling in its drowse.
Not these she sensed — nor needed intervention
In her frail stand. She watched her life
Passing before her; jugs and buckets and jacks
Of living water.

IV

Children kept in. Doors locked,
Eyes at all windows —
The sky would fall! Prisoners off the farms
In the well field, picking the flowers!

A birthday in their camp
Or someone dead? A shocking sight!

Waiting the bus that collected them,
They swished the grass
With tired legs, they laughed like boys.
One — older, ridiculous —
Paddled the stream, gathering iris.

These men had killed our lovers,
Vandalised homes.
From sanctuary, we glared —
War's women. How could we allow them
To need flowers?

71

V

Gone, under gorse...
The golden enemy, forever watching
For the scythe to stop hacking,
The feet to stop coming,
Ways to eradicate
Ways that had been...

'When gorse is out of bloom,
Kissing is out of fashion'.

Today, one blaze of gold,
Dark wind-shafts under.
The water-voice escapes
Out of the hood
But no one hears or sees.
Lives upon layered lives,
Walking their paths at proper times

And our irreverent ease,
Meaning no offence, finding the field
Beautiful. At war's end
We left, for good.
All but one of us...

The cat was elderly, whose paws and tail
Defiled the sacred place. He, too,
Gone under gorse.

Stillborn

There was a child born dead.

Time has bleached out the shocking insult,
Ageing has cicatrised the body's wound.

Still I do not like to prune bushes
That push to the sun...
Nor put my brush into the spider's house
Where she keeps her children,
Darting with terrible life.

With reluctance, I gouge potatoes
Sprouting intently in a dark bag.

Furtive, I slip one into the earth.
"Grow!" I say. "Grow, if you must...."

The Carpet at the Barbican

Across a glowing ocean
Of carpet, we tow shopping
To a sofa in a kind of grotto.
Other sofas
Scatter as islands, peopled
With oblivious lovers,
Loners, drifters from time-of-day,
Above discarded shoes.

Galleries rise
Up and around, en route
To the great musics and the plays.
We are here for our feet.

Far down the carpet — a whole venture-cruise —
A sign says, "TEAS."

Suddenly, a boy
Cycles in from the world
And wheels, and goes,
Back into London. Look — no hands!
He is black and beautiful
In a leopard-print catsuit —
Impudent but, like surrealist dreams,
Perfectly natural.

We stroke for our tea
Over the flowing carpet
With its tidal mandelas
Then tack back, to our haven of sofa,
Mesmerised voyagers....

Glimpsing, at sea, five little men
Turned breast to breast in a tight circlet,
Singing to break the heart; rehearsing, no doubt,
For an imminent concert. Their folk yearnings
Thread us with mood — as though the carpet
Undulates waves of patterned
Loneliness, from them to us
Who shop and kip and splurge
Our public loves
Each on an island: whose long homes
Will not be more secluded than these sofas,
Freeports,
Along these wastes of carpet.

Visits

Our daughters spoil us,
Bringing such offering as made our day
In childhood. Naughty comforts,
Warm, entertaining chat,
Promises.
"When summer comes..."

They overdo it; because now
Our darkness looms, in which their eager news
Or anxious moods — equally confided —
Will fall handless.

We will not be here.

They are unaware of this dread.
It is an ache
They never touch — like the hurt knee
Of infancy, or the first shame.

We smile. And take.

Backgrounds Observed

Peering, in depth,
Behind the lovers, murderers,
Intriguing corpses —
To lamps, ornaments,
Even a cushion like one of ours,
Backfill windows
Rushed with Hollywood rain....

Are these things meaningful
To the enacted scene? And, if so,
Why seldom noticed?

Is it to do with differences
Between truth and fiction?
Rose gardens, panelled rooms,
Enhance Jane Austen serials
Like a bodice trim, taken for granted —
Yet documentaries
Advance their settings, as binoculars
Feather a nest.

Therefore, surprised, behind Kim Philby's shoulder
We spy that cabinet
Of fine china. And one of the 'boys'
(So-called) who created the Bomb...
Svelte as they come, with a lovable grin...
Fronting a hedge we might not note
But for the contrast
With his terrible presence. Such delicate blossom!

A La Carte

Freshness between stones. Noon stuns
An underlit bell
Between sea and sky.

Neap tide.

And the flatworm rises,
Geared for the lovely act
Of symbiosis: seals into itself
Particular algae. Sea-light activates
Fused translucence. They blend their need
To mingle with each other
Not as merging factions,
Incandescent lovers or fierce insects do
But in elegant anneal — cool,
Perfect in accord.

When God feeds —

And surely, His designs
Must nourish Him? Do not we all
Consume symbols of our power? —

He must be spoiled for choice
With a whole universe
To whet appetite.

From primal soup, peppered with meteorites,
On to protein (the creatures forming)...
As side dish, might he not prefer
Flatworm — innocently drunk
On salt light —
Before humanity? Always so cocksure
Its gamey tang must be His favourite!

Faithless Dreams

Sometimes, in dreams, we meet our souls'
Perfectly matched shells,
Linked at the dreamer's hasp: shone through
With heat glowed from a lucent dark
Between curves. Even while we coil about
Sleeping companions, the shells close,
Melting the quick.

Sense of the ridiculous,
In serious dreams, deserts us.
I and this civil servant (bowler, umbrella)
Phosphorescent nudes on a station
Clocked with farewells. We were not sad,
Knowing we'd meet again. Other disguises —
But the dream, basic.

Once, drifting to a wedding,
Early; the dream confused with miners
Going to work. Catching them up,
He walked with me, instead. Nineteenth-century
Pit gear this time. Cap over eye.

The sun rose remorseless
Over village and mountain. We lay in the shade
All day. I never got to the wedding
Nor he to shift. Married (he said)
And I, Promised.... Yet we were guileless
As Dante and Beatrice, young and untouched.
I, in her red dress...

We need not value our homes and day-loves
Less for it; nor feel guilt on waking...
For surely, those with whom we share
Beds and sleep, also have their dreams?

To Father and Mother

When you return in dreams,
You smile, you are never cross with each other.
On the bizarre picnic, the fall-away cliff,
We dream together.

Often the fogs of war
Clogged my young breath, often you stood
Like two lighthouses, stabbing your powerful beams
Crosswise above my head.

You always smiled at me,
Never guessing at my built-in radar —
Hear beyond hearing, say nothing, think huge
(Children, the world over).

Your parent joy in me
Was not enough; I wanted you to smile so
One to the other — partners and relaxed,
As in finding mushrooms.

Now, in dreams, you do.

Valkyrie

(For E.B.)

Too young for love, we shared an opera score —
 'Valkyrie,' misprinted translation
Of a German libretto.

What green-and-golden fits of desire
In that room shadowed by trees,
Shaded by disapproval
Of our stubborn affair....

Laughing, we'd meet each other's hands
On the sultry inserts. "He overcomes her *scrumples*
And they embrace." Joke over,
Passionately grave, we too embraced.

So long ago — and still I catch, with dread,
A footstep at the door.

You never heard that step. Your fascination
With 'Valkyrie' would cloud your eyes
Blind to the thwarting problems
Of courtship; drawing my perturbations
With you — adoring, dutiful
To your hands on the keys and serious beauties.

You were never like other boys.
As I think down the years (more than sixty, now)
Always a succession of fires,
Flowers, music. Through tough times —
No matter what — I see you coaxing flames

In me. Bonfires and beach fires,
On a broken hearth, deep in a stove
So cheerful heat came out, opening up flowers
That you'd bring in, even on dark days,
From our string of gardens.

I don't see you old
But building fires to charm away cares,
Finding me flowers, keeping the old score
For its misprints....

Once, on an autumn day,
Whistling 'Valkyrie', you called a robin to us.
We lived, at the time,
In a wartime shell of a house, making do —
Desperate, sometimes. When I look back,
Mostly, the robin comes, tilting indignant
With his elderberry eye.

It is the bird I see.

Confrontation

At the cliff edge,
Accepting autumn: no more drawn
Down to the high, impetuous tide.

The twenty-first of September,
At day's end.

Stricken by sunset. Trying the life's
Evening mood, what equinox brings
Of change, surmise,
And, between crimsons, the angry greys.

Everything happened where the work was caught
In the excited hand —
Insight, the splendid messages,
Arrogant craft....

How bright the workplace was!
Such dazzling light,
Often one could not find the tools
Or nerve for stumbling towards them.

Round the illumined cliff
Assessments flounder —
Sanguine then dry and cold,
As on this sea-blown bank
Skeletons of campions turn, in the coloured wind.

from *A TRIAL OF STRENGTH*

Keeper of the House

I live a good lie.

In my house, we are three queens and a king.
And why not? The weather is cold.

They say the wild bee
Lasts out the long gales with a cell each side
Of sweet cloy. The banter is kind
In the king's room, he never dreams
He is not a king

And here, the clocks and all the mirrors say
It is happy spring.

I have a soft tongue talks
To the drawn curtains and the dead projects.
Such a talent! My honey sticks down
All the weakly wings, we do not conceive
We can never fly.

What is the use of knowing? It's warm in here
And I live a good lie.

What do I Stand for?

When I consider the night battles and the day cries
Out of my strings, corebones: the one luminous drop
From the distilled dreams — now they seem meaningless
As rejected seeds, bitter as samphire
Tasted in blowing salt,
Sadder than monkeys' eyes — these flares out of my heart.

And yet, I glow. I burn with the best leaves
In the gold-shouting wood. When children laugh,
All the blood blooms in my consort of pipes,
True as a rose. I am made well with love
And colours tell me their right names, their secret names,
Complimenting my stand in the world of lights.

Why, then — since I wear joy for a shroud,
Must all my shinings celebrate the dark?

At the Big Stone

We were like silk-lined gloves,
Softly turned inside out and shimmering,
The seams that bound us stood up lightly proud
Of the loving shape,
A double-edge of May

When, in crescendo, every quickened force
Ventures beyond its frame —
Transcends the boundaries of wing
Body and eye and legs of climbing sap,
In understanding of the May morning.

The big stone stirred with us in the field.
A haloing force ran all around his silence —
That never leaves the core, except in May,
On a May morning.

We had linked hands on his rough slope,
One with his glow-green sweat and emanations,
Small snails and lichens, reviving fern.
His difficult aura, looping about ours,
Sighed up and outward through the primal stone,
Pale, gentle as the haloes of gems.

The big stone has always been here,
Pitched along earth. A landmark.
We see him strongly when we think of home
But had not thought stone was a word for love
Until we shared his consciousness of May —
A shine out of the stone, embracing us,
Ritual...

Elegiac, too...

As though we understood the May
With weaker lightning afterwards,
The emerald gaze
Stone-heavy, tired.

Whose elegy? Whose?

A Time to be Born

Do you ever lie awake and hear the world turning —
Knowing quite well, there is no such sound —
And does it comfort you?

Often we listened to the world going round,
When we were young and close, unsure
Of our deep intimations. So the developing foetus
Feels the mother's heart beating its future
And is programmed to wait until her blood says *NOW*

Through the ring of the world sustaining its constellations
In balance, is thin and high —
Almost beyond the mind-shell; not like the human heart.

We slept at the time in one of those white rooms
Out of a Russian play — seemingly empty.
There may be simple clutter but it feels
Furnished completely with the bed's shadow
On the moonlit wall.

There were phases when the very sheets were
Statements in moonlight
Of all we might become. Possibilities hovered
Sweetly above the silvered floor
As new-opened leaves float into movement,
Euphoric, effortless —
Spoken from the hard stem.

Yet, many a night, darkness confused the certainties,
Black, thick, silent as the twin grave
We sometimes spoke of — should our strangeness undo us.

Then we would hear the world turning,
Telling us — to wait.

The Healing Woman — of her Gift

Many keep gardens of herbs.

What comes into me goes beyond herbs —
Nor is it a matter of being called.
Any good neighbour will answer in trouble,
Taking old skills along
To childbed or sheepfold.

I scarcely heed, at the time, what close-gone thing
Has been chosen to use me —
Only to void the force which, suddenly rising free,
Turns me, as a whole tide to swim a fish
Dried up in mud. As a huge rock fallen,
Crushing a snake....

It is not myself,
But that which comes into me.
Afterwards —

If I have gone some way, finding that work —
I can hardly get home.

No one will touch me.

Sometimes my father will come from the house and help me
In, to my bed.
I lie for three days,
Sweating the intaken darkness out of me.

I can go back then, to cleaning the place, knitting,
Minding the fowls. Perhaps for long...
It is not every day, nor every year, that God sees the necessity.

We always live so quiet; it's lonely here.
My father will throw wood on the fire,
Speak to the dog. He has never said
That I ought to get up and cook his supper,
Instead of resting....

And I never ask if he knows what is wrong with me.

The Storming of the Castle

This life met anguish many times....
Learned to contain, like bladder or like gut,
The waste of dream within a private envelope.

A hard and last lesson; a final project.

For like an animal or a young child,
In the preliminary pains, all was thrown down
For the world to share.

"Look what has happened!
See how I suffer!
Hear the strength of my cries!"

While for the last lesson, a dignity
Of stones, or the widowed swan,
Came in to home. The inordinate, loud
Unprivate combatant
Preferred silence.

Time

In the twilit room, flung about on chairs
Difficult to rise from
For shape and the wine passing and the four men
Such old friends....

Discussing time,
Its nature and implications.

One had the very latest time
Under his tongue; but the tip was slowed
By this reunion. Others ticked louder,
On wrong strokes. And he grew heated.

The woman without philosophy
Stayed by the window, watching degrees of dusk
Trigger the engines of moths.
She fetched more wine: otherwise, dumb.

And the more they minded about time, the colder
Flashed the brain-stars in the warm faces
Trapped in the chairs....
Until one face altered. He who had the gist of time
Sagged and flicked out, taking his exposition
Into a black hole. How they upstumbled!
Chairs overturned, feet ran, the conditioned room
Seemed a wild cave. Ambulance lights
Made the moths a flare-path. It was a torrent of time.

The woman without philosophy,
Stunned,
Caught herself in a mirror collecting glasses

That had begun full,
Varied in depth and brilliance,
And were all empty. It was now day —
That had been twilight, and then night.

And she was slender and voluble once —
It had not mattered then
How time did: what time was.
She said — feeling a dream state. "Time is change?"

Village

In this old village now, at night,
Towering above, the strange sodiums point flares high,
Blanching the street; all shadows fled
Back, back, under these potent organs
Into our doorways, making them dark hoods
From which emerge mauve faces — as though dead.

When we lie down, the sodiums burn through the curtains
Into the rooms, scorching our oldfashioned sleep.
Great tankers fly
Corrosive liquids, the simple milk
Frightened in loud drums, enormous decks of sheep,
Hurtling down the Roman road.

We think we hear the sheep cry —
It is the memory of a sound, we have not really heard it
For some years — so hard and swift they roar now
To their morning deaths. And we seldom cross the road
Into their fields.

The sun rises: but the sodiums take over
Sunset. Woods, and the village tree,
Glare as in pantomime. When the river breathes
Into our evenings its familiar mist
Scented with grass and sewin, all those homely vapours
Suddenly turn a sickening red.

Around this time, the mauve dead patiently peer and gossip
Under the hoods.

At the South Pole

This book is my link with Father —
Whom I never succeeded in meeting
Though we looked at each other.
Generation photographs show our like eyes,
Clouded and wide — the same secretive head.

Through childhood he wore this book,
Passed down to me. I put it on.

Inside the dark-blue cover,
Separately in our ship we have both served.
Mind into mind, the gloomy engravings
Quickened and sailed, through auroras of lonely lands
In the childish acceptance. Inherited under a seal
That never broke, between Father and me,
Into mature smile or the laughter of friends.

We feel our tall, our grinding, tall ship's arc
Wildly raking beneath the Cross. The cabin boy's clingings
Loosen and fall. The cruel captain stands,
Eternal blackness and crack ice in his least word.
Pointless endurance. Of coming madness shriek the Horn winds.

Now the wrecked crew hones across wastes,
Roped on each other, dragging attempted salvagings,
Beating for shelter. Intrepid mate
Saves little cabin boy from mesmeric clefts,
Opening. Closing. Opening. Under engraved sleets.

Father and I have watched the albatross
Trusting the thermals. He turns his beak.
Above the glowing turquoise of the berg,
Together we count the feathers of his neck.

The Picture of the Tiger Hunt

I did not wince because the tiger is pinned by spears,
Stuck and lifted on the elephant's tusk.
Nor for the blood too bright
Nor for the forest leaves
Streaming to blaze the scene,
As in frightening dreams.

No; what moved me was the tiger's hands.
Hands — not paws —
Past all powerful dealing,
Sprawling out wide, loose,
Asking astounded of the continuing spear,
Of the red workday gleam in the elephant's eye.

So do all creatures, peaceful or tiger, lift hands,
Not paws,
At the flash of death.

This picture was done by a 'naive' painter.
'Naive', we call him — and we look for truth.
Hands open and shape NO! Hands, not paws.
Two or four hands — or one, as in a dying flower.

Towards light is the last appeal,
And should evoke tears.

One Man's Answer

I know now why my hand moving in yours
Yet cannot tell you all I want to say.
Why some are striped with lions — or a mind of wood
Clamps to a sweet headpiece. And again, why
Some work with slithering force
Akin to fishes; others make love like spiders....
And the great western skyflags burn to sing
But crimson has no voice.

I have the answer now. Nothing is wasted.

Nothing is wasted in my house or the house of life.
All things — *all things* — die into a mingling flux.
No perfect form comes out. We are marbled with one another,
Flinging a pattern, from confusion spun
Out — and far out —
Lovely and orderly as a grebe's breast,
Oh, unimaginably farther than Orion...
Laced with some radiant chance.

How did my child come by that hyacinth look?
Her parents are dark, little people, without shine.
She was caught in the flow of a recycling spring,
While her new making swept and was gathered
In with this chance. One in the other born,
One in the other dead. Nothing is wasted.

I first knew this when lying along a rock —
While from the inland fields and the town dump came birds
    of the sea,

Planing above my upturned face
To the night raft of birds in the headland's shadow
Where was night already; but the underfeathers and the feet
Fluting their webs, were lit by the low sun,
Birds of gold. So are we all homing in
To the night-resting sea, one in the other
Fading and lost, recycled. Lit with the sun
That is dying also, into its chance. Nothing is wasted.

Since I knew this — it does not matter, why.

Room for Manoeuvre

If the tide is always out
When you go down,
What is the answer, the right ploy?

Do not try catching it in coves
Difficult with stones.
The sea draws farther out
Over a broad sand and the mud desert
Will blaze out silver
With light from a big sky
As you wait for the turn — searching
Where the starfish sucks the drained floor,
Cockle and seaworm sipper
Delicate kilts, the razorfish protrudes
His cautious longhouse, all enamelled white,
Trembling ozone.

Into such vast escape, it is safe
To feed your loving. Why not stagger sleep
So that the tide is sometimes in
When you go down?

Sometimes is often enough
If you choose open skies,
Belling up tints, blooms — but not in coves,
Where skies are merely tongues
Between rocky claws, giving no quarter.

In sufficient cloud, a love can tear slow places
For blue-reflecting eye. It finds a grace.
There is nothing sudden, it will match moods

Over the shimmer of mud, to yours that favour
The far-out edge where the birds ride.

You will be warned of the coming tumble and sluice,
You will hear the birds
Before the powerful seas invade.

Notonecta Glauca (The Water Boatman)

The water boatman,
Cox of his own hindlegs,
In silken rhythm rows his world of ponds.
Road-catch of standing rain,
A field shallow with a dangerous bird
Or the village mirror
Where people on seats
Puzzle the negatives, their self-soft sepias,
Doubting their truth.

But water boatman, rowing upsidedown
(So he conducts his life),
Knows through the tenderly fitted pane of his pond
The helpful sky —
That free gift scarce a recipient blesses —
Of which he keeps a pocket in his wings
For his deep situations.

Time behind time, beyond and before time,
Has refined his oars,
Adding hairs for a wider sweep
And to carry air-pearls into the pond's dark cup.
Always, where foods and perils lurk,
Breatheable sky goes with his legs,
A spare sky-bubble reassures his wings.

This is so tidy, one could laugh — but marvel
His tuned antennae, feeling out for trouble.
Radar he must have — so his adapting head

Posits the sensitive probes, streamlined in holes
Beside his eyes. Together they use the free sky
And let no news impede his bursts of flight
From fancy to fancy of his ponds.

The Tea Party

I asked my dead to tea.
Accumulated news pointed my tongue
Like a pin through silks, like a crammed bee-bag,
Heavy to unload.

They sat in the garden,
Smiling the stone-burnt roll-call of their names.
I set a table between roses,
Laid with their favourite things.

Oh, my sweet dead — the cakes, the cakes!
All news discharged to the faint, receptive sheen
Of your listening eyes. Then, for the first time
I knew that you were dead at last, and I —

Healed?

It came upon me with the emptied teapot
And the westering sun. I had no plans for you
Beyond the afternoon.

The Heart Tattoo

Always looking for a later place,
Walled round with rock, a beautiful grey.
The completing circle of sky
Dreamlessly pure, colourless, without intervention
Of cloud. No sound
Except my heart, resting.

A whole life resentfully at war. Mouth to mouth,
Eye against eye, the wrung hands, the involved breath
Never full-drawn...
And always looking to the final place
Of neutral alignment.

Yet, in my afternoon,
A tentative sunset pending, ushering in the truce,
I found that, owing to such strong experience,
I was indelibly marked with my enemy's pain.
Could not cleanse or disown it — would never curl
Into the my-size, impregnable keep of rock,
The sanctuary —
But must carry the world because I knew the world.

There is a wonder in it,
An unsought grail cup,
A dark, embittered, honourable drop.

I can say, with one who also was imprinted
By wounds of others, that could never heal,
"On the way to the place where I wished to be alone,
I was taken ill."*

    *Reputed to be the last words of Tolstoy.

from *THE INTENT LOOK*

Home

When the flawed apple is cut
And out of it, the red spider —
Minute, almost too small to be noticed —
Runs desperately across the tablecloth....

Desperately?
This is to load spiders with our own dark,
The round black pit into the apple

Home.

Desperately, because
If the red spider finds no substitute
For lost home,
There is built-in running to do, without pity.
Over the desert cloth,
Between hot cups and rolling crumbs,
Mountains, avalanches,
Till the legs find death.

Nonsense! so slight a speck will quickly find refuge,
Without much running.

But then ... the cloth is shaken.

This is a sensitive day, we cannot decide
Whether spiders function by circuit or despair?
Dispossessed, we too will react like the spider,
Hunting for a site —

Mating. Eating the outworn mate.
Running —
Frantic afraid —
Dying.
Losing home after home.

So like: yet however closely we identify
Nothing fractures the walls between species,
Nattily papered with repellant skins.
Layer on layer
Between the running red spider
And desperate human spider
Who has eaten mates and lost homes,
Running, running all the way.
After the running, death brings us sharply together
As though we were all one print

And so we are
Once we find home.

Trying the Cruel Forms

I need to be of my time...
So that I stand, to the end, primed and aware,
Feeding bonfires. Of my time. Clear.

Towards the clanging of the shocked instruments
Placing my large hand — on the strings, to feel
Discord and fray
Flung up and out, up and over, by the bow
That has no choice but to continue
The rocket concerto.

But there is nothing I can take away
Into darkness or rapture —

Nothing to remember.

Trying the shapes again,
Closer to the skin, under the nails,
Hard —
As though digging through quake-earth, —
Does not help me with my afflictions.

The outbursts are amazed in wrong order,
Never repeat, echo, under closed lids

Nor do the manifestoes make me any hold
Against death.

Must I, for saving spinshafts
Out of the mind, always lean backward
On old patterns? Imprints and presentations

Of worlds that were indeed life
But had not death

Not as we live it.

Those singers and magicians
Created antidotes to the deaths we had then.
Life's journeymen could take the tools about
Like bundles children carry or clutch in sleep,
Full of sustaining treasures.

I could reach so far, to be of my time...
But the deaths are too formidable. Without love.

Leningrad

There was this woman at the officers' house
By the winterset port.

Cooking, cleaning, looking after clothes —
Moving so silently in her felt boots,
Never speaking, unless addressed.

Our men would say, to new arrivals,
"Irina came all through Leningrad!"

And she was truly proud of having survived.
A wound of dignity would open her face
Before it healed back into the leather mask
Of a woman whose family — sons, husband, father —
Had not survived.

We asked her, once. How had it come about,
Her survival? How had she managed to fool
Death? And she very simply said

"I have eaten cats and rats and have drunk blood.
When it comes to that — you enjoy them all."

Scrapyard Woman

Derelict farmhouse
On wasteland
Shot by Inter-City.

Glass flash
Sound flash
Silence.

After the shot, drips
Echo, in openings
Still upthrusting pegs
For harness and tools.

No look-out
From the end window.
Against that, the car mountain
Heaps, tangles, sings
To the shot bullet.

Afterwards, mute.

She is much alone.
The inglenook dog (with eyes like hers)
Is from some other time.
He appears for the foul burning of sleepers,
Combustible junk with an oily smoulder —
And lies down
And is company,
Though the thick of his body
She can see the floor.

After tea, sometimes,
She wanders beneath sunset
Over the waste land.
Thin golden grasses shine
Above found objects
Again rejected. The willow herb
Breaks in its roseate cry
Against Inter-City's
Hard seam.

Jumped hazards of wire,
Rhines of lurid water —
She is come to that stage now
When the dog follows her

Far from the tarry inglenook
And piled cars.
Sunlit cooling towers,
In the sky like gods,
Offer complete forms.
Towards them she runs,
Clumsily beamed
Through accidents of light.

Over known fields the dog runs with her,
His bark
Making no sound.

The Magic Number

Once, at a festival, I saw two together.
Brother and sister? Lovers? Their spines hung supple as feathers
From their proud heads. What could it matter
Who or what they were — king and queen, I named them,
Of a land inherited at such sightings,
A youthful, unploughed country.
Royalty colours that simple earth,
Moving like willow wands.

Trying life's early holds,
Often lost, mistaken —
I found in a book, casually opened,
The young Chagall and his wife

Turning away from us
Into a radiance....

And what that is,
Where it goes,
Is felt as a migrant thing,
Sunlit —
That will come again.

Revelations, assurances —
We tell them out in the dark all our lives,
Lose and find them by turns
And, as a blind man know them
Guides to a centre. Brilliant white sticks
Probing a way in to the land held in common
But possessed through symbols.

For me, the vision-pointed two together —
Whether the unknown folk dancers
Or Chagall and Bella....

Singer and song, matched in melt,
Can sweep the rivers of that country
Over such magical falls!

But the girls at Lissadell, in the silk kimonos,
Two together
In later years were drifted into one
I trusted with their beauty.

My gazelle.

'The shades of evening, Lissadell.
Great windows, open to the south —
Two girls in silk kimonos,
Both, beautiful...
One — a gazelle.' —Yeats

A Neighbour's House

I live both here and there.

While I sit making my poems
In a window, the south visits that roof
In full silver, wonderful....

Shalom.

I saw a bird stripping moss
From the tiles: her mate with her
Croaked encouragement. He did no work,
Which went on all day. In the end
She could not carry any more for the nest
But flopped, wings loose, recovering. It was then
The bared space, naked to the south,
Bloomed silver, bright as a dazzled sea.

Since she is gone who lived opposite
And told me her life,
Her house has been mine
As things may become ours
That are done with in their present form
But will bloom dark or silver
With the weight put on them — of bird,
Brightness, or simple looking
Of one in a window, hidden.

She was a tall old woman
Of a stripped serenity.
I feel through the silvered tiles
Into her time — the children she had lost
And her husband who liked cutting thumbsticks

For friends at the mart.

I strip my poems.
The south comes; and the moon
And a young man knocking down walls.
He is making the house over,
Fiercely he wrestles beams, partitions.
Coming already tired
From a day's work, he batters on.
I have to crouch behind Busy Lizzie,
Lest he notice and think, "What a gawp!"

Throwing back hair, he scuffs with mad purpose,
Mixing cement, shovelling rubble.
Sometimes, his two boys
Whose home he conjures, trot about
Quarrelsome, playing ball.

Young man, I wish you every good.

It is not your property
I take over, to inhabit secretly —
But the outworn life,
Willed to me by deeds not of this world.
To do with hands round cups
Brimmed with our common fears,
To do with looking at what life is,
Together.
Catching one long breath.

Her lost sons will never appear to your children.
Nor shall your roof be blinded by my south.

Two Rhondda Valley Poems

1. 1926 Strike

How sad, the rag-and-bone man's horn
Lifted on high....
Tooted with a wry neck,
Sidewise from his flat cart.

The sound hung on afternoons
Of few blackberries,
In littered dingles where we played.
Men picking coal on tips
Caught the tinny blare
Coming and going. Gone.

Blow to the heart,
A known mock. Women listened
At closed doors.

Rags... and bones...

2. Living With It

After certain weather,
The bracken purpled
Dark and beautiful, to the moraine colour
Of people's hearts

That broke, slowly,
Hidden in bone and decently.

Managing mostly without weddings
But at funerals showing
Close purple,
Slashed with iron's red.

Old Tips

Over the years, a tip would take on time's finish,
A greening over —
Seen from far off, a patina
As on bronze memorials. It was a feature
Of place and weather, one of the marks of home
To my springloaded people.

Autumn in the allotments; sunlit on high,
The town shadowed. All the pits asleep.
Sometimes, cows off a neglected farm
Would stray across a very old tip —
Lie around on the strange, wispy grass,
Comforting their udders.
Old tips breathed out a warm, greenish smoke
After rain,
Suggesting thin, volcanic pastures.

Some tips were famed as wicked, secreting runnels
Of dark, treacle death; swallowing houses
Helpless at their feet.
But most were friendly —
We children ran out of school
Visiting the one that rose
Close to our playground.
We scrambled towards the top —
To shriek the dandelion flaring in the grit
And that abandoned crane,
Pointing to the annual sea.

Whatever is There

In the streets, these days,
Around parks and shops,
Many walk hand-in-hand who once would have gone
Arm-in-arm
Or simply side-by-side...
Not necessarily youthful, beautiful —
As those who have always sprung hand-in-hand
Towards the future: whatever was there.

I watched a couple on the wintry shore,
Enduring their promenade. Husband and wife
Who had grown old into each other
But were not friends. They wore their limitations
In a separate carapace, their voices resounded
From pebbles. Still they went hand-in-hand,
Forgetting they did so, clinging to the finger twist
For dear life.

The sea roared, far out.

Then, at a green man crossing, the walking bruised
From a Sheltered Home. Hand-in-hand
As was only sensible.
These were fully aware,
Despite their cloud (or because of it)
Something was there.

It would seem, on a crowded Saturday,
Love has come
To one and all, twined on the handmade rope
As they choose meat or buy a souvenir....

Overdone women,
Men whose belligerent eyes
Foretell the coronary. Fearful to move apart,
To be caught lonely with the sensed alert.

And the sky holds calmly above the city
A hint curled west at the edges. It will be night.

Only children do not go willingly
Hand-in-hand.
They wrestle their innocent force from the mother's grasp
And rush ahead in delight,
Shouting to their heritage.

Whatever is there.

The Garden Girls

During the 18th and 19th centuries, women of Wales — especially in
Cardiganshire — used to migrate to London to work in the parks.
They were known as 'Merched y Gerddi' — 'The Garden Girls'.

Movements on a land — single
Then run together like ants, wildflowers.

The great Bog. The sky.

Spring migrants, following paths
Of the Old Peoples.
Banks crusted with cattle hairs, the Roman roads
Under rain and sun.

Wave, to the hill farms, hanging down poor fields....

In wake of the drovers; on foot, by pillion and cart,
Skirts excited beyond prudence, eyes shining
Above mud and dust with the excitement of it....
Some had been before and knew the ways
Of London streets, roundabout to the green parks,
The market gardens.

Others wore hard work and honesty
For a Welsh hat; on the strength of those
Went up in the world, never looked back.

A few were immortalised as strawberry sellers.
They smile at us out of rhyme, out of old frames.
Short season — yet the scent of strawberries
Carries an image of pleasure, always in fragrance.

And some hid homesickness in shawls,
Weeded the sunny hours, came home pregnant.
For such a one witty song was made,
Nobody now remembers...
She, and the child, and they who sang,
Under stones.

The great Bog remains,
Shrunken. Birdcalls she would have known
Lost into change. Certain pastures
Gone under plough; like the unfeeling song
And the old ways. And the Garden Girls,
Spending their summers.

Visiting the Collection

Often, in galleries,
Those delicately bright pictures
Light would fade
Hang between sheets of hard protection

As with memories, dreams.

A hand moves to swing the beauties forward —
The case
Rattles.

Or they wait behind curtains
Of occluding stuff
Such as a Quaker uses, or a nurse,
Hardwearing, practical as common day.
A gesture twitches this aside —
What translations revealed!
Even the non-colour of tears
Fresh and immortal.

After many visits, no necessity
To read labels. Instinct will choose.
Perhaps he sitting in a dusk, head bent.
Above him, the same picture (but unprotected)
Furnishes that room. The heart feeds.

Or the shield's transparent, a mere dust-cover —
Thus a child's joy can be looked at always.
The laughing face endures whitest light
Forever....

There is one glory of the moon,
Another glory of the stars.
No need, really, to lift a hand,
Only to glide between shields, curtains...

The honed edge of choice
Instantly inserts.

The Arch Rock

Father and mother. Light shines them in to the child,
Confusing the eyes.

She is on a rope so that she shall not fall.

Cliff slides under sandal. Dry flowers
Scrape the small hand — dry blue nodders.
Ticking like watches in the burnt grass.

"Come on — on — on — on...."
Cries the father, already echoing
By the promised sea.

Has she done something wrong?

She is on a rope so that she shall not fall
To the dead gull washing through the water
By the Arch Rock.

And the path narrows, the mother wedges her body
Past an overhang, the wind balloons her blouse
Bluer than the sky.

The Arch rises off a beach
Confined in shadow,
Made of cold little stones.
There is a cave where the mother stands
As in a dark house.

But the child shines between mother and father —
Brightly! Brighter even than she can!

While the live gulls rise with rough clangour,
Beak above beak stabbing the cramped sky
That is the blue of bewilderment.

The father is swimming through the Arch Rock.

Why does she remember how light said
And they said nothing?
Light flowing out from the Arch. The mother standing.
Tide flung high up the stones, the father bleeding.
Blood on the sky blouse. The rope trailing...

"She shall not fall," said both lights, shining like earache —
But in the top of the head, an interception
Of rock statues. The mother speaking
Out of the cave, as when the child
Once told a lie. Speaking to her
Or to the father? The child was not sure.

Through the Arch (and brought the dead gull nearer)
Came a huge wave.

The Intent Look

Quizzing an old face can overprint youth
On the craggy droops, Intent fancy
Conjures a mouth's uptilt
Towards life-lit eyes —

Coming, gone again. Coming —

Till the old face wins.

It is a vice, this fascination —
Like scraping for money on sacred ground
Or disturbing a pupa, to spy metamorphosis
In holy cold, of the sprung changing-space.

In mirror prisons
I am constantly willing
Lost contours to haunt me,
Overlying this mask
Which is (I hope) a late form of chrysalis,
Soon to transmute with splendid instructions
Each visiting face.

I need to know!
Are these the larval stages,
Called out of my folder of weathered skin?
Is the kept secret of the caterpillar
Mine also? I am, though human,
A very imago for readiness —
And so much bolder
Than caterpillar. Ruthlessly,
Faithlessly bolder...

Once, in a needle of looking,
I split a chrysalis through
In its calm privacy, to catch the nature
Of *this* to *that*.
Then, I was wearing
The youngest of these faces that come and go,
A child assassin

The chrysalis surprised me.
It had nothing to show but a drop of golden water.

Birdwatcher

The wagtail taps his exclamatory endfeather
Over pocks in the road.

Who knows what primordial drum
He lives and taps to —
By which we also are vibrated
And no longer notice

As we accept heart's contract with blood.

A bird so light —
Tacked on air as a few pins to a veil.

The important feather weighs him to reality.
Tripping round potholes
After ghost ephemera
Misted up into the humid weather.
Such minutiae, sprays of electric dust,
Answer a chiffon tempo.

Once they are delicately picked
Into the wagtail's bosom,
Their haze must coarsen in time
With his microcosm, many powers larger.

They will become steps in his dance.

Endless, the pattern and repeat
Ringed, echoed away like stoned water —
Out from pin heart to universal pulse
Steadier, stronger with each absorption

Of primal dancing: towards whatever
Coils the whole into vast unawareness

Utterly restful.

As graded feathers of cloud, vaulting
Pale to hot bright, beat over beat
Fanning to luminous climax.
Must we ask more?

The wagtail does not.

from *VISITING LIGHT*

Woollen Mill

What we are hangs upon that moment —

Which *will* come —

When the cross is taken in the warp
And the weave is certain.

On the drying ground
Where the wet wools were hung to blow,
Scarlet, blue,
I was first aware of a true pattern.

To do with light....

It was an overwhelming addition to myself,
Seeing, prepared in light,
How the warp lay. I had to go and sit down
Behind the carder, trying to come to terms.
In the pile of fluff lay a dog, asleep.
Between his half-closed lids
Light sparkled — even there,
In the dreaming eye.

Down the mill walls, light translated water,
The roaring silver
Over the wheel, that ground out light — and light —
Danced out of ancient cogs
From when they were young wood.
Such bright looking hurt....
When someone passed
I turned my head for relief of his shadow.

But he left two fish
On the window sill — and they burned light,
Drew it into their stillness
Like a great cry. Blinding silver.

The man dressing a loom was all afire
With fused intent, passing down arms and fingers
Into his skilful moves.
As in a thrown shuttle
I watched the visible mix
Between his light of mind and the silverlit water
Working outside. At that time
The mill was run by water, in dry weather
The wheel stopped; but then,
Against such interval, a mountain of wool was dyed
Scarlet, blue —
So that when rain came and the wheel turned,
There would be plenty of wool ready
To take the cross.

It was that season when the natterjack comes
To water, carrying her mate
(Or so they did on my far-back nameday)
And as they processed,
All the light in the sky flew
To touch flashpoints where the webbed feet
Displaced moisture — tilted instant mirrors,
Killing all dark places
Between flowers. Marsh buttercups — and those
Fill up with light, even in thunder.

Look back, from evening. A widespread day,
Maddened yet silked with light.
Toads assembling,
Wool blowing unbearable keen colours,
The two fish burning
Scissors of light. The weaver took them home
To his shut house. The mill shut down.

I suppose every turn of the earth
Is loom to someone's light?
A skein untangles
Out of wind and sun,
Lies in the ordered warp, patterning
Scarlet, blue.....

The cross taken.

* A stage in warping a loom is known as "taking the cross".

145

Peter, Dreaming

Peter considers much, how it will be
Not to be: when no one is left
Alive on earth. He and his mates,
Brash in their time, bypass the shabby deal.

Accept....?

Nightly, inside the owl-skull
Strung from a poster of Burning Spear,
Some creature starts its count-down —- sinister
To a boy's tidal mind
At the flood of reality. Peter has accepted
More than his age can bear
Without tender naps. He dreams
Bursting asunder of the world. Sleepwalks
The small hours, clicking at retakes
Of the nuclear film.
Cramping on stills
White as flashed bird-lime —
Risers and strugglers
Fractured from each other
Into stunned solo. Thousands together.

Yet they are all one person —
Peter.

In the hedge once, a wasp nest
Potent with grubs. "Keep well away, Peter,
There may be fumes."

But the examined frame was beautiful —
Roughly heartshaped; not in flat emblem
But as the full heart in a body
Ample....
Layered in hexagons, each one a home
Perfect for wasps. Angry, but not evil....

The whole geared to the future of the grubs.

Where's the dynamic force of world-parents,
Dedicated hordes
Organised fiercely as wasps
To save Peter?

He dreams his father, clumsy with poison,
The deep, arrested groan
From the hexagoned heart....

Silence.

The Source

Today has been like a shoe
Fitting too tightly,
Pressing a penitential band
Over the toes: not to be eased off,
Because today required just such a smart
Disciplined shoe.

Once, I saw Auden creep
In his mapped detail, out of that kind of day —
Back to America.
Early on, he had taken a small bag
Out of his mind and, during the formalities,
Kept it close to his surreptitious leg.
A well-used bag, blazoned ADIDAS —
Couldn't have held much. Some lifesaver
For these occasions, a sponge, a few poems?
Perhaps — his death?

My bag holds always the same panacea
Against the test of pinching shoes and days...
The certainty that — at any moment,
However fraught —
Severn rises in Plynlymon's wilderness,
A handful of water stealing away
Through the lonely brown...

If it is not evening yet,
Evening will come.

Sorting Jumble

Respite here. Escape here.
As newt in pond
Feels the uprising springs
Bubble, prick, against its suspended form.
"Where are you, why don't you jump? ZZZZZZ...."
But the newt's camouflaged. A stone.

Stand-easy here. Chair folding its ruin,
Frayed and faded rug — that was *too* red.
Redundant books —
Once their students wore them
For hats, umbrellas; and are now fit
To run their minds naked.

A gauche plant, banished for eccentricities
Of growth — unacceptable
Between smart curtains —
Sprawls relaxed. Nothing more expected,
It may branch birds, clouds.
There is sufficient silence.

Unassailed here. Yet a woman called
Who had lived in this house.
Describing her family's childhood,
Where the sideboard stood, where the piano —
She said, "Two brothers died
In the room where you sort jumble."

Must I elude their deaths — sad boys
Whom I never knew?
Pricing stopped clocks, tired woollies,
I hear their hearts...

The springs rise up. The newt comes alive,
Pricked by the inescapable world.
Those boys may play with any
Books, clocks, umbrellas that they choose.

On a Performance of Noye's Fludde

And when music told us
The Ark was ready,
The town's children came
In heads of lions
Bears, owls — each animal and bird.

Two by two. Hand in hand.

Their feet on the aisle floor,
Trotting in rhythm,
Thudded like heartbeats.

Why were we so moved?
Was it to do with God
High on a wall, steering the goings-on
In a big, necessary voice?
The children-animals taking so long
To reach, without loss of heads,
The belly of the Ark....

We ourselves had contrived
The brute masks — paper and paste.
When they began to run, they came alive.

Some of us wept.

Perhaps the very simpleness —
Clunking a row of mugs to express
Imminent storm. 'Kyrie Eleison'
As a tribal dance. *Was* it so, once,
When we were children indeed,
Under God's horns?

Tight round the crowded Ark
As we could get, roaring the "Praise God"
Not as a hymn,
More as a splendid yelp
After dangerous work,
The children-animals
Herded to sanctuary. The tempest quelled.

Dark, outside.

Further down the carpark,
The nuclear bunker. A few still staging
Comfortless protest,
Most of us sick and tired
Of the politics. Back at the church,
Helpers already dismantling
The cardboard Ark.

Visionary Aids

Never seen
Because never thought?

A way, some thread not pulled through the maze
Though it shine level with the eye.

Sight reinforced by thought
Can work miracles.

Go on — glare, furious enough, at smoke
Lazy from the power station!
Billow it, speed it —
Rolling bouquets of carnation,
Another sunrise, if you like,
For the sullen street.

Fierceness of thought was all it took
To do that.

But eye neglects (without slow camera),
How when a drop falls back
Into milk, into grief's wine,
Impact forms a beautiful small crown.

Other exquisites too, things unfolding
Precise being — not at all what they seem
To the unaided glance: a world behind the world —
Once found,
Everything there jewels the looking.

In slowest-motion thought, a seeing comes
That finds us out...

As when it seemed sure, by illumination,
Trees at the full are aware of God...
All day, their tranquil intake focussed
Centring absolute leaves: the tripod extended,
Exalted, from off the earth.

But, night...?

No human eye can read the dark
Unless it uses the eye's own afterlight,
Magnified by faith.

The Fox

Lightfoot on loneliness,
A winter fox

Not hunted
But as the true light in fur is,
Each hair a spirit
Of the whole radiance.
Light and the woods
And revelation
Come all together, as though prophesied.

Later, in weariness,
I dreamed a fox
Running on sparkle. Delicate tread
Indented trackings of mastodon,
Dinosaur — back and back
To infinity's edge. And there, the fox sprang off
Into the dark. I saw his diamond brush
Illuminate nothingness.
These imprints faded,
Fused into man's with links of holy fire.

This was the long-expected comet,
Emanuel. God-with-us.

I had not thought
To see that in my time — and was asleep
Only a minute.

Walking Home

A room in a bishop's palace,
Diocesan matters
Discreetly filed, stencils....

In winter, sometimes,
Sunset pouring through an oak — so old,
Arms are chained to head. It flares indignant,
Glinting its bonds. The typewriter answers,
Simmering red.

Why not such fancies? Machine and I
Have done the work, meticulous —
No less efficient
Because sunsets change us.

It is, that lonely tasks
Breed fancies. Years of walking home
Through the great garden have enriched,
Saved — perhaps from losing 'strangeness'?
Delicate lens
Tinting the common sight, quickly mislaid
Among computers, systems
But in a musty room
Facing the freedoms of birds and squirrels,
Become an intuition; grace to see
Natural lambency about the creatures.

Some say that people emanate
This shining, also. I never saw it outline
Any that I know.

Therefore, it follows — walking home,
I am not luminous to birds and animals   (15
As they to me. My passing means no more
Than the shadows of firs
Brushing out a cold evening coming.
Fir shadow too, in the brown room,
Very sweet all day. One must ignore it
For the work's sake. But afterwards, what harm
If the shadow perceive a sudden flush
Between unhuman things...
The oak, the typewriter
In its business mask.
Were not its steely vitals drawn
Native as oak, from the hot earth?

A thousand blackbirds roost
In the drive bushes. Garden and churchyard
Are one broad round, steeped in ceremonial
Long before Christ. Often I feel the rites
Quilling like blackbirds....

This is an old, holy place,
Waging perpetual wars. I side with them —
But am unsure under what rising powers
I walk home

Looking In

A documentary
About a desert. We sit relaxed,
Unshaded eyes learning that torrid floor.
Marvellously graded stones —
Head size to ball size
Through pearl-small, fining to dust.
The killing wind
Over and round them sings —
We are in the heart
Of the maelstrom, without being blinded.

Then, to switch off, go out....
Tonight, a mackerel sky,
Graded crescendoes of fleece, away
To diminuendo. Serried beneath the moon
Motionless shells, pearls....

Could we position the cloud
Over the stones,
Might the completed jigsaw
Point us a sudden strike
Into eternity? As when
Leaves and birds and a companion's hair
Blow all one way — a chord
Brightly sustained, then slipped
Like a forgotten name.

Sit in again, for the News.
March with this evening's people,
Out in world thousands, patterning
Grief and excitement, fear —

Graded from huge 'O'
Through the extremes of hate
To dying aperture.

Note what intricate lace
The seismic needle vandykes,
Screening an earthquake's passion.

High up, an aircraft
Scanning the devastation
Photographs jigsaw truths
Of a city's death
Repeats the needlepoint's
Fairylike art to shock,
The dainty chaos.

Still Life: Flowers and Greens

These thoughts
Are the deep jug of water
Where the flowers rest; far enough away
From the roots' cry.

Circulations, systems
Curving, feeling with one another
Not as we humans curve and grieve
But in their closed dimension
And wild stillness

Synthesised only
By the small gaze
Of the few, groping to scale away
Evolved eyelids, to glimpse, clearly,
Something other than thought-babble....

As between varied grasses
Glancing their plumes,
Between shadow and stem
On a windless day —
The faint pulsation.

These thoughts
Are the tentative link
We sometimes move to express
But our mind cannot. Never.
Loud as we are in loss,
Hot and unkempt in our human wounds,
Numb to translate
How roots communicate
Mutilation.

Still. Silent under sun and moon —
Green and the flowers of green,
They have not long
To be their own. Taken in and done for,
Turned into flesh, into dung,
Changed, for our use
And the upkeep of animals.
So harvest goes,
No help for it. Why should we fret
For what we must consume, will snap loose
To decorate our tense forms?

Churches
And geometrical rooms.
Brides.
The dead...

Wife and Dolphin

Sunrise gulls, each one glittered
On a raft of diamonds. The loosed rope
Shimmering...
And out between Cradle and Cat
To bait the pots. Brooding there,
Alone in the boat.

A hot-tempered man.

Sometimes, he saw his wife's face
On the water glare. He had struck her a blow
And she had left. Would never return —
That was her nature.

Lip tide —
With a light haze, lifting —
Was her eyes' very colour. The gathered sea
Loomed, whitened, parted on Cradle and Cat,
Foundering over.

He would chat up the dolphin
That was pleasant with him.
Had it play stick
Like a dog, watched it take fish,
Flash, swallow — jokingly neat. He dived once
Under the silver flump of it,
Touched his hand to belly and flick,
Smiling snout.

It became his own —
But free, he wanted that —
Looking for him to sight and amuse it.

He, too, was entertained,
In morose depths delighted.

Saving for a new boat,
He would take summer people out
To see the dolphin. Two went with him —
Showman types —
He soon guessed they had plans for it.

What to do? Temper made trouble.
When he was sure of their intent,
He would go alone
Where the full greenswing
Sets away from Cradle and Cat,
Far out...

And play stick with the dolphin —
Hit it hard on the nose,
Hard. It would never come back.

That is its nature.

Every Day

Every day, something is given —
Even on black day, blind day.
As though a force —
Itself immune —
Indicates sudden balsam,
Consolation. Pain may continue
But the spirit lifts.

If only this flower —
Year on year, in the bare, northlit place,
Raising a single constant
Of piercing blue

Which may mark the grave of an angel
Such as (a visionary tells us)
Die all over the earth,
Not divinely protected
Like the great angels.
These patrons stand for us
Unarmoured.

Every day, some dissolution of fear —
A bright hand
Sweeping icicles: instantly lost
But seen: given.

Even today, so bleak and rainy
We pull curtains and watch an old film
About jungle nature — the want of colours

Blessed with perceptive mirth,
Noting a leopard
Enfold her child — with the moon look
Into her paws, of a human mother.

Shutting the Book

Up and down the tired Valley
He roared the old bike

When he had petrol.

Every girl's friend,
No girl's lover. Little legs
And the beak of an eagle.
A hunchback.

In those times —
Old folk just looking on, the young
Sticking up out of their foundations
Like blunted nails —
His black jokes, his sunny smile
Bits of the bike tied on with string —
We laughed beforehand
To hear him coming.

In the hall, for dances —
Never dancing.
Singing up at funerals
As though death were nothing.
At the shotgun weddings, standing best man,
Grinning a future...

One of the girls, leaving
To find work, cadged everyone's picture
For the album, was given his quip
In token. "My *photo, love?*
No, no — you'd never be able
To shut the book!"

Visiting Light

A single rose-red tile
On an opposite roof
Comes and goes among adjacent slates,
According to light, weather.
Rain, blown off the spring river,
Brings it up proud
Of surrounding greys —
Like an expected face, flushing.

Roofs fascinate —
How they straddle families,
Equal across the too-many
As over the so-lonely,
Giving nothing away.
Discreet above violent stoves,
Cold or much-tumbled beds —
The small saucepan with one furtive egg,
All he can or all he will
Allow himself — which?

Here broods a latent poetry
Nobody reads.
The weed that has managed flowers,
Pinched in a crack,
Lays its thin shadow down
In the afternoons; as a new mother will,
In the room below.

Jackdaws are in these chimneys,
Their difficult lives
Reflect our own; but who will be awake

For the luminous dawn
When the young fly for the first time?

Jackdaws seem inimical
To the mosses, disrupt them down
To me, as I clean my step,
Rubbing with bluestone in the old way.
My scour against the world's indifference
To important symbols — the common roof,
Likeness of patterns.
How warm this moss is,
In my cross hand! A miniscule forest
Full of see-through deaths
That should have had wings....

"Under one roof"
Is such an old expression,
Steady and parental —
Yet life beneath,
Hidden by the roof, changes pace
Daring and malicious as jackdaws,
Unpredictable
As visiting light: or the one rose-red tile
Flushing up — vanishing.

Nothing — and Something

At the house corner
A cling of cat hairs
Stayed up on breath of noon
Rising and falling —
Tongued out of her garment
As she rolls in flowers.

She, too, is the colour of marigolds.
Of this cat's mark upon the world
Nothing visible save one eye
And, up there, the catch of hairs
Gesturing. Wider than a web —
Which would be common to the wall,
Part of it. This fanciful weave
Becomes the question
Bloating all things discarded.

It opens like a cage,
Streams out in tension —
Stretches a pure Picasso throat
Towards light; then falls,
Limp from the point of catch,
Succumbed.
For an instant, the breeze lent it menace,
Reproach. The lazy watcher made of it
Delicate outline of a face.

What is the fate of such a cast-off?
Which for the dreamer, sketches on air
Attitudes: of a lost cause,
A poem out of time,
That face...?

If it outlasts winter
It may become involved
With a nest — highjack a seed.
On days like this, millions loose parachutes...
Or cripple flies
Of the finest small-engineering precisions
That yet, hardly ever, know the way out.

Or the hard rains may purge it thoroughly
To the wall roughcast
And for such likely fate
Again the throat shapes poignant —
An anguished net flung about
Places of the mind
Without sleep or hiding...

The cat emerges from the marigolds,
Her silk trousers
Tacked with ruined ephemera,
Displaced ants.

Solva Harbour

Always one hill brilliant and one dark,
In memory — sharing the long curve
To sunset. Seas leap and fall
With a white sigh around two rocks,
Markers and exclaimers
Under whatever sky,
As we are ourselves

When we return, to breathe upon
Fading light. Is such remembering
A life form? Will it revive
Peripheral presences?
Floaters in the iris,
Vague to central vision
Dazzled with happiness....

Forms we would now acknowledge, name
As witnesses: whether or not aware
On that day, how we sat stunned
In our own silence, like the boats
In the emptied harbour,
Waiting for inflowing tide
To move them again.

There was a girl running to swim
In the evening: she would be old now.
We scarcely noticed her pass
But the years insist, she was beautiful.
We would recreate her
Out of the mindless joy
Through which we sensed her....

She: and the flowers in our colours,
The seabirds. All we did not heed
Being on that day our own
Adamant life. In a sunned mirror,
Brighter than experienced...
Though it blows up for storm
And the harbour's grey.

The Companion

I, too, had a companion once,
Such as you describe — an unseen certainty,
Tactful in its stay.

At a time of bewilderment, winter.
Big child moving her small child
Endlessly between house and school,
Up to the shop and back...

Breathing for head room, heart room —
Clinging beyond reason
To the small child's hand; yet mute.

What was there to say?

The sky enormous, hard with fast clouds,
Daws falling in purple wheels
Upon the oaks. Storm hanging
But it would not break
Down from the thunderous head
Into the heart.

Then I was first aware
Of someone with me —
Always a step behind,
Keeping me company. As soon as I was sure

The rain fell,
Strong convlusions of silver.
The child played outside it,
In a blackberry dry

And the companion shielded her
While I raged.
I slept, afterwards,
Still as a chair, by the evening fire.

Time has done much; a late spring
Loosening all that ground. Coltsfoot rising,
Sun beside penny sun, as on wires to light...
Small child grown. Big child's foolishness
Seen to be growth also. Company plucked
Out of the very air of anguish.
Who was it that came —
Under the storm-cloud fetched
And from the cleared sky gone?